C. The Arts;

i. Art History

MOVIE PALACES

Wiltern Theatre—Los Angeles, California

MOVIE PALACES

BY AVE PILDAS

TEXT BY LUCINDA SMITH

FOREWORD BY KING VIDOR

Clarkson N. Potter, Inc./Publishers NEW YORK

DISTRIBUTED BY CROWN PUBLISHERS, INC.

For Emma and George

First published, 1980, in the United States by Clarkson N. Potter, Inc.,
a division of Crown Publishers, Inc. All rights reserved under the
International Copyright Union by Clarkson N. Potter, Inc. No part of
this book may be utilized or reproduced in any form or by any means,
electronic or mechanical, including photocopying, recording, or by any
information storage and retrieval system, without permission in writing
from the publisher.

Clarkson N. Potter, Inc.
A division of Crown Publishers, Inc.
One Park Avenue
New York, New York 10016

Published simultaneously in Canada by General Publishing Company
Limited. Printed in Japan by Dai Nippon.

This edition has been produced for Clarkson N. Potter by Rosebud
Books, Los Angeles, California.

Designed by Ave Pildas

Library of Congress Cataloging in Publication Data
Pildas, Ave.
Movie palaces.

Includes index.
Moving-picture theaters—United States.
I. Smith, Lucinda. II. Title.
NA6830.S63 1980   791.43'0973   79-14485
ISBN 0-517-53857-1

Acknowledgments

Grateful acknowledgment is made to the following:
Don Ackland, Bo Hathaway, Bernard Schleifer, Beth
Rashbaum, Jason Niiya, Pentax Corporation, Bill Hertz,
Mann Theatre Corporation, Noelle Soren, Architectural
Historian, Missouri Department of Natural Resources.
Sarah Shelley, Executive Secretary, League of Historic
American Theatres. J. H. Vandermeer, historian, State
of Washington Office of Archaeology and Historic
Preservation. Joe Dusibella, Terry Helgesen and Brother
Andrew Corsini, Theatre Historical Society. The Los
Angeles Public Library.
And a special thanks to S. Charles Lee.

CONTENTS

FOREWORD BY KING VIDOR

My first job in the world of movies was in 1912 as a ticket taker in a nickelodeon theatre called the Globe, in Galveston, Texas. Perhaps it should not be called a theatre in the true sense as it was in fact a converted music store. The conversion was accomplished by moving all the musical instruments to the front of the narrow room and installing a partition into which were cut appropriate openings marked Entrance and Exit. The tickets were sold by the proprietor at the guitar and banjo counter. The price: ten cents. I sat in the darkened room just inside the curtained entrance arch with nothing to look at but the picture on the screen (which, by the way, appeared to be a stretched bed sheet hung on the wall). Just below the screen sat a pianist at an upright piano. The complete show took only half an hour, and the program was changed twice a week. My hours of employment were from 10:30 in the morning until 10:30 at night. I watched the original *Ben Hur*, an Italian film, twenty-four times a day.

Gradually the running time of the films began to expand and so did the size of the theatres. At first local opera houses and music halls were brought into service, and the prices rose to twenty-five or thirty-five cents. They then soared to seventy-five cents for a special road show production in which a full orchestra accompanied the silent film in addition to the regular theatre organ.

The desire to capture the willing flow of every public dollar began to express itself not only in the growing splendor of the films, but also in the competitive magnificence of the Movie Palaces themselves. Across the country, theatres began to rival each other in decorative opulence.

When I first arrived in San Francisco in 1915 (via Model T Ford), D. W. Griffith's *Birth of a Nation* was showing at the Savoy Theatre with an eighty-piece orchestra. The film and the theatre were in competition with the grandeur of the Panama-Pacific Exhibition then in progress in Golden Gate Park. For me, at least, it was the exhibition which suffered most by comparison.

When I moved on to Los Angeles and the heart of filmland—Hollywood—Griffith was already in production with his next big picture, *Intolerance.* Hollywood had as yet no large theatres important enough to exhibit these great epics, so we had to travel the big red electric trolleys to downtown Los Angeles. The trip, the films, the theatre, the large orchestra all made it an important event, one to plan and think about for a week or two ahead. If we felt we could afford it, we had dinner at a downtown restaurant to complete the gala.

The principal feature film was generally preceded by a newsreel, then a two-reel (half-hour) comedy with Chaplin, Harold Lloyd, Laurel and Hardy, or Mack Sennett. Then came an overture by the orchestra which blended into the lowering of the house lights, and the start of the feature. And if you don't believe that the lavishness of the Movie Palace itself added to the subtle magic of the silent films, I wish you could try it sometime. A truly transcendent experience, and one that has not been duplicated since, was created by the ambience of all these appeals to the senses. So entranced was every member of the audience that no one ate popcorn or unwrapped candy bars. The viewers were so lost in the total effect that they could not take their eyes from the screen or the decor to indulge in a little necking or whatever else goes on in ordinary movie theatres today.

In subsequent years we made many excursions to the Million Dollar at Third and Broadway, the Paramount on Sixth, and Tally's on Hope Street. Monday night at the Orpheum on Broadway became a regular social event. On this evening an entirely new vaudeville program began and tickets were at a premium as most big Hollywood names attended opening night to see and be seen.

Lights flash and neon whirls to welcome James Cagney's *Yankee Doodle Dandy* to the Warner Theatre in Hollywood.

Dick Whittington

By the early twenties I had been making films in Hollywood for several years. They were mostly short-run entertainments, the kind the studios wanted, and I began to feel that they were not compatible with the grandeur of the great Movie Palaces. I went to the executives at Metro-Goldwyn-Mayer and told them that I would like to make film that would play for longer than the week's run customary at that time. They gave me the go-ahead on the first anti-war story written for the screen. Opening in the Fall of 1925, *The Big Parade* played to sell-out audiences for two years at the Astor Theatre in New York, and for six months at Sid Grauman's Egyptian Theatre in Hollywood. The film was accompanied by an eighty-piece orchestra plus a crew of eighteen stagehands creating the most convincing explosions and special effects. This entire extravaganza was booked as a road show with similar engagements throughout the country.

Sid Grauman, proprietor of both the Egyptian and the Chinese theatres, was known as the "master showman." His penchant for producing elaborate stage shows which preceded the feature film was a source of irritation to many directors. One might attend the opening night of one's own picture and see several scenes from it reenacted on the stage by an unknown and untalented cast, greatly undermining the impact of what was to come later in the film. For a long while Grauman had a fully robed Bedouin character, illuminated by brilliant spotlights, walking back and forth along the flat roof of his Egyptian theatre. And when Douglas Fairbanks was starring in *Robin Hood* at the Egyptian, Grauman had an actor on the roof with an unbelievably resonant voice boom out above the boulevard traffic, **"Robin-Hood in Holly-wood!"**

Then came sound and dialogue, and the viewer could turn away from the screen for long passages and miss nothing because the sound track would keep him aware of what was happening.

I will have to admit that many things have altered and expanded the horizons of filmmaking, particularly the advent of sound and dialogue. But nothing was so exciting to me as the experience of the early silent films shown within the gorgeous surroundings of the Movie Palaces. A magical experience has been lost and I can't imagine the likelihood of its ever happening again.

INTRODUCTION: BEFORE THE FINAL CURTAIN

Come enter a world of magnificent refuge from the everyday—a world of glittering splendor, now virtually forgotten. Within opulent auditoriums, people watched their dreams come to life.

The Movie Palace provided an environment of total escape where its patrons could lose themselves in a fantastic world of architecture, music, and larger-than-life personalities. Lights, colors, posters, and an air of excitement greeted the public. Lined up under a dazzling marquee, moviegoers could indulge their fantasies with pictures of favorite stars such as Gloria Swanson, Rudolph Valentino, Clara Bow, and Douglas Fairbanks. For the housewife who attended a matinee or for the couple who watched an evening performance, the Movie Palace represented a spectacular vehicle capable of transporting them into a magical realm of make-believe.

There was too much to see in only one visit. As spectators passed through the shiny brass doors, the elegance of the grand foyer would seize their imaginations. The enormous staircases, five-story marble columns, hand-woven rugs, and gold-leaf cherubs tempted them to return again and again, each time to marvel at a citadel whose colossal proportions had been created solely for their entertainment.

Next they entered the lobby with its original oil paintings, fine antiques, and exotic images of mythical gods. A legion of ushers—precision-perfect hosts of the Movie Palace—would break their astonished spell with the wave of an illuminated wand and direct them into the auditorium. Seated in red velvet comfort on plush seats with hand-carved arms, they joined perhaps five thousand other guests in an ornate pleasure dome decorated with the lavish intensity of the Palace of Versailles or the Taj Mahal. The Movie Palace was easily the most splendid structure most patrons had ever seen, and the experience had cost less than one dollar and was right in the center of town.

The show began when a spotlight focused on the magnificent Wurlitzer organ. Dwarfed by his instrument, the wizard at the keyboard produced romantic melodies to enhance the mood created by the stars glittering in the atmospheric ceiling overhead. Then, in a more up-tempo mood, he accompanied the audience as they "followed the bouncing ball" and sang popular songs of the time. Under the glow of a golden proscenium arch, the orchestra would then rise out of its pit on a hydraulic platform and launch into a rousing selection such as the William Tell Overture or a Tchaikovsky concerto. This eclectic program might then continue with a musical number complete with dancers dressed as bathing beauties, flowers, or drum majorettes. Meanwhile, lest spectators forget their palatial surroundings, each time an act would change, the illumination of the auditorium would once again enable them to admire the awesome decor.

Captioned newsreels came next with scenes of President Wilson pleading for the League of Nations, Jack Dempsey battling with Gene Tunney, or Charles Lindbergh landing in Paris. A musical solo sung by a handsome tenor, or a trio performing a sentimental recital might follow. The cavalcade would continue with trained dogs, seals, jugglers, or Spanish dancers. Although it was not necessarily the major attraction, the silent feature film was generally presented last after a long series of live entertainment. The film was accompanied by the organ or by the orchestra and was frequently followed by another musical selection.

When the lights came on to stay and the stars faded back into their concrete sky, there was still enough time to mingle out through the Byzantine arches, past the cascading fountain, and take a last visit to the magnificent French powder room. Visitors caught a glimpse of posters for the upcoming attraction as a uniformed usher said good night. Reluctantly, they strolled out the door, under the marquee, and back into the procession of humanity. It was somehow easier to

The stars came out for the gala opening of Benjamin Marcus Priteca's Warner Theatre in Beverly Hills on May 19, 1931.

Dick Whittington

face the boss in the morning or come home to a crowded apartment when you knew that next week or maybe even again tomorrow, you could go back to the enchanted world of a Movie Palace.

History

The penny peep show has remained one of the last great American bargains. For the price of a single copper coin, a viewer is momentarily whisked away from reality via a series of photographs or animated drawings. This primitive machine still fascinates children in carnival and amusement park arcades. Once a scientific toy, the peep show gave birth to a multi-million dollar industry, and its simple thrill ultimately changed the history of entertainment.

Its principle was described by Dr. Peter Mark Roget (of Roget's Thesaurus). In 1824, he explained his theory of vision in relation to moving objects. This concept, also known as persistence of vision, maintained that the eye could connect individual pictures when they were projected successively and could interpret this progression as a single continuous motion. Even though Greek mathematicians and Leonardo da Vinci had experimented with this theory long before, not until the nineteenth century did scientists grasp it and set about developing an apparatus that could utilize it.

Throughout Europe and America, scientists continued their experiments with the "photographic memory of the eye." In 1889 Thomas Alva Edison and his assistant William Dickson invented the Kinetoscope, and the word "peep show" entered the nation's vocabulary.

The Kinetoscope was an elementary device that presented fifty feet of moving film to an individual viewer. Edison had originally intended to combine moving pictures with sound but following the success of the Kinetoscope, he discontinued further experiments with the "Kinetophone" and continued to produce one-minute silent films at his Black Maria Studio in New Jersey.

By 1894 penny arcades with Kinetoscopes were popping up all over the United States, and because Edison had neglected to pay the $150 international copyright fee, peep show parlors were making news all over Europe.

On the site of what is now Macy's Department Store in Manhattan, but was in 1896 a dark and stuffy little building called Koster and Bials' Music Hall, Edison unveiled his latest invention—the Vitascope. By projecting the Kinetoscope's images onto the wall, the Vitascope changed entertainment from a private experience to a show for an entire audience. Films of breaking waves were so life-like that front-row viewers feared they would be drenched.

Movies became a popular phenomenon so fast that there wasn't time to construct buildings exclusively for showing them, and since the public seemed more excited about novelty than concerned with comfort, many shops converted into theatres and small businessmen made small fortunes. In order to make room for the hypnotic new toy, merchandise was shuffled up front and floor plans were reorganized. Long, narrow spaces were crowded with as many uncomfortable wooden chairs as possible. Most store shows soon gave up their previous business, but a few still sold goods. Infrequent customers would make purchases, their shadows momentarily interrupting the picture. Colorfully printed banners advertised the poor man's show while the upper classes walked by and turned up their noses, hoping that the novelty would soon wear thin and life could get back to normal. But, with continuing innovations in the technology of movie-making, the comfort and aesthetics of the theatres, and the sophistication of the story-telling, movies were here to stay.

R.C. Reamer's Fifth Avenue Theatre in Seattle, Washington, displayed a gilded assortment of Buddhas, dragons and Chinese lanterns.

In spite of the excitement caused by the initial novelty of the movies, audiences soon grew weary of the theatrical-type films which contained only one scene portrayed on a set-like stage. In 1903 however, crowds were back in line at the local store show to see Edwin S. Porter's *Great Train Robbery*, a Western that not only had cowboys, guns, and bad guys, but told a story and created suspense.

In 1905, in a tiny converted store show at McKeesport, Pennsylvania, two ambitious partners, Harry Davis and John Harris, raised the price of admission and gave their theatre a name. They took the cost of a ticket, combined it with the Greek word for theatre, and called their show a nickelodeon.

Movies were more than a rage. They were a business that in the early days was dominated by ambitious local entrepreneurs. Even though the movies were the main attraction in small towns and big cities, they were still regarded as a working-class diversion. Not only did upper-class audiences avoid the movies, but sophisticated businessmen stayed clear of the Vitascope and therefore enabled early theatre owners to prove that their grass-roots intuition definitely paid off.

Gradually, more comfortable chairs and a few decorations improved the spartan accommodations. Before potential customers paid their admission, they could look through a tiny hole for a glimpse at the theatre inside—the original sneak preview.

As the theatres became more appealing, the quality of the films also improved. The public's insatiable appetite for entertainment created the motion picture industry. Each time attendance fell off, the filmmakers, entrepreneurs, and businessmen were forced to develop something different to get their straying audiences back.

In 1915, an actor-turned-director named David Wark

Griffith broke away from the tight clinches of Thomas Edison's Motion Picture Patents Company, which had controlled all film operations until then. He made the legendary *Birth Of A Nation*, a film which made cinematic and social history. D. W. Griffith developed editing into an art form, and when he combined his innovative close-up shots and camera angles, *Birth Of A Nation* aroused emotions in its audience never before imagined possible from a motion picture.

With the number and quality of renegade independent film producers growing, the foundations of the monopolistic Patents Company crumbled. Out of its ruins arose the studios and the star system. Fearful of the power stars might assume if the public learned their real names, the Patents Company had refused to let its actors be known by anything except the nicknames the public gave them. Independent producers however, realized that even though an actor might demand higher salaries, the public would be willing to pay more at the box office to see their new idols. When Gladys Smith went from "Little Mary" to Mary Pickford, a precedent was set. If stars didn't get their fee at one studio, they would take their astronomical demands elsewhere. Actors who had been making from five to fifteen dollars a day before 1910 could demand two thousand dollars a week five years later. By 1917, Charlie Chaplin and Mary Pickford had individual salaries of close to one million dollars.

Movies had become big, big business, and producers as well as actors were making fabulous incomes and leading the kind of lives that made front-page news.

While the nickelodeon and cramped store-show theatres were adequate for the working classes, amenities more spectacular than wooden seats and a clinky piano were necessary to lure middle-class audiences into the theatre. On April 11, 1914, Mitchell and Moe Mark opened the Strand Theatre on Broadway in New York and began a whole new era in movie houses. The Strand was a far cry from the crassness of the nickelodeons. Audiences who came to see the movie also saw crystal chandeliers, gold leaf, and art work. Escorted to their upholstered seats by uniformed ushers, they sank their toes into plush carpeting with every step they took. A ticket cost twenty-five cents, but in addition to a movie, the price included a chance to hear a thirty piece orchestra and a mighty Wurlitzer organ.

When the theatres were upgraded, the movies became respectable. Prior to 1914, the height of an elegant evening might have been a visit to the "legitimate" theatre, but the Strand proved that Movie Palaces offered stiff competition in elegance, as well as a stage show and a movie. In 1912 few high-brow actors would have considered going into a movie, much less performing in one, but by 1915 the movies had immortalized many greats of the New York and European stage.

Movies had arrived, and at a perfect moment. People were desperate for entertainment and hungry for news of the war in Europe. Once the newsreel was over however, they could relax and momentarily forget their problems. The war effort had consumed the attention of many European filmmakers and consequently the responsibility for entertaining the world was placed in the hands of Hollywood. In addition to Charlie Chaplin, Mary Pickford, and Douglas Fairbanks, Western stars like William S. Hart and Tom Mix were providing audiences with romance and adventure.

The end of World War I saw the beginning of an unparalleled flamboyance. There was money to spend, things to buy, and the freedom to dream. The decade of the twenties was a time to exploit affluence, and the Movie Palace stood out as a shrine to this indulgence.

With the pressures of war removed from the public

consciousness, a general easing of America's traditionally puritanical attitudes took place. Once the producers sensed this more permissive mood and new curiosity, sex was added to the plot lines.

By 1922, sex was on the screen. It was also flaunted in the lives of many of Hollywood's biggest stars. Under the strict supervision of Will Hays, the Motion Picture Producers and Distributors of America was organized to get the industry back in line before it faced national censorship. A compromise was reached. Sex could remain on the screen, but a moralistic ending was to be added. Cecil B. De Mille removed his camera from the glamour of the boudoir and in 1923 made an epic called *The Ten Commandments*. This extravaganza had the blessing of the Bible plus the bliss of wickedness and the sanction of remorse.

All across America, housewives went to the movies to gaze into the eyes of Rudolph Valentino and take his memory back to their kitchens. They studied the vamp techniques of Theda Bara and Pola Negri, hoping to work the same magic on their husbands. For thousands, the cinema offered a world removed from their daily lives, a world of glamour and magic. Motion pictures fed the imagination of the masses. By showing them what was beyond the familiar, the movies altered existing attitudes toward courtship and marriage, and also invaded provincial enclaves with knowledge of a broader world.

Prosperity in the twenties seemed within easy reach. If you wanted to build a dream, financing was at your fingertips. Credit became a popular term and debt a familiar way of life. More people were going to college, and the movies illustrated the rewards of success.

New conveniences were placed before the public that allowed them the freedom to expand their lives and contemplate new ideas. Money could be spent on a wide variety of fashions, appliances, and entertainment. A family did not have to be rich to own a refrigerator, electric mixer, vacuum cleaner, radio, and washing machine. For many Americans, the twenties were like Christmas morning: a great big grab bag filled with wonderful presents.

Mass production dominated industry, and its most important product was the automobile. The average person could do more than just dream about the things he wanted and the life he wished to lead. He could jump into his car and go after it.

With all the energy, mobility, and leisure generated by the twenties, the movies offered a logical place to go. Dressed in the latest fashions, people would climb into their automobiles and go out for an evening of fantasy. Newspapers expanded to include entire sections of movie-star gossip and each star had an enormous following of fans.

The movies encouraged a variety of goals. The films of the jazz age inspired young women to emulate the fads, fashions, and mannerisms of Clara Bow and Joan Crawford. The attainment of money, sex, and beauty became the new American dream. Every man wanted a wife who looked like Gloria Swanson; every woman wanted a husband who possessed the manners of Douglas Fairbanks.

Film stars were the high priests of the twenties and the Movie Palaces their temples. The European monarchy took centuries to develop, but the celluloid aristocracy of America attained royalty overnight.

The Entrepreneurs

Many entrepreneurs adorned the landscape with their versions of the Movie Palace. At best, they were mere imitators of the legendary man whose name is synonymous with this tabernacle of the twenties: Samuel Lionel Rothafel or "Roxy." Even those who have never visited either the great Roxy Theatre or the Radio City Music Hall have undoubtedly heard the word "Roxy" for it is still used to signify a place of magic, a touch of class, and an era of elegant sophistication. Samuel Lionel Rothafel was the supreme impresario of the Movie Palace. He was one child designing the playhouses for many millions of other eager children.

Samuel Rothafel was born in 1882 in the tiny town of Stillwater, Minnesota. His father was a shoemaker who moved the family to New York's Lower East Side hoping to find more work. At the age of sixteen, Sam already envisioned a world of fantasy which so annoyed his father that he was asked to leave their house. Rothafel took off in search of his dreams but landed in the Marine Corps. As evidenced by the degree of regimentation he would later demand from his theatre ushers, he obviously learned much from the pomp and discipline of the military.

Following his hitch in the Marines, Rothafel joined a minor league baseball team and picked up the nickname "Roxy." By 1907 he had embarked upon a new career as a book salesman. Stopping one day for a drink in Forest City, Pennsylvania, while traveling his route, Roxy made a decision that changed his life. He took a job as a bartender, married the boss's daughter Rosa, and persuaded his father-in-law that the little tavern was an ideal spot to introduce moving pictures to Forest City.

Roxy wasn't concerned that his first enterprise was on a small scale. His mind was thinking far ahead and Rothafel's Family Theatre became a miniature laboratory in which to research ideas about lighting,

The legendary master of the Movie Palace: Samuel Lionel Rothafel, "Roxy."

Courtesy Terry Helgesen

stage effects, and audience reactions. In no time at all, the folks of Forest City were regular customers, as were some curious visitors from other towns.

After working for a short time with vaudeville producer Benjamin Keith, Roxy was asked to rescue the ailing popularity of the Alhambra Theatre in Milwaukee. He assembled a regiment of ushers, taught them manners and dressed them in uniforms worthy of their role as guides to the newly-emerging world of fantasy which Roxy was creating. To add to the flash he took the orchestra out of the pit and put it on stage.

Even at the outset of his career, Roxy dared to be spectacular. The movie theatre industry, at that period of its development, was like virgin clay, and Roxy was its master sculptor. One can imagine the young entrepreneur lying awake at night unveiling to his patient wife Rosa the wanderings of his imagination and how someday they would lead to Broadway.

When Henry Marvin hired him to salvage New York's floundering Regent Theatre in 1913, Roxy knew he was on his way. Not only did Marvin want a spectacular theatre, he wanted it constructed for the sole purpose of showing movies. Roxy was ideally suited to such an assignment, having spent the previous six years developing his ideas about the proper environment for movie-going.

Roxy was also a skilled and intuitive musical arranger, even though his formal knowledge was rudimentary. Stirring music dominated his theatrical program. He recognized the essential importance of music with a silent film and insisted that the accompaniment relate properly to the story. Before a movie opened at the Regent, Roxy himself scored it. Throughout his career, music was more special to him than even movies.

Roxy was a master of entertainment. He recognized the public's hunger for spectacular escape. By creating a total environment for his audience, he put them in the mood for architectural, musical, and cinematic art. He was also the perfect host. The public was his guest and he believed that from the moment they first contemplated going to the theatre their entertainment became his responsibility. Even from the highway, a Roxy marquee had to offer incentive enough to lure the public inside. From the moment they purchased a ticket, while visiting the lounges, or when watching the show, the public was there to enjoy themselves, and Roxy wanted them to return home feeling better for the experience.

The race was on for each new theatre in New York to outdo its predecessors. Roxy had no real competition except himself. From 1914 to 1920, he moved like a conquistador, seizing the Strand, Rialto, and Rivoli.

Another who fancied himself an impresario was Major Edward J. Bowes. Bowes was a partner in the awesome Capitol Theatre on Broadway. With its mahogany paneled lobby, crystal chandeliers, and silver leaf domes, it was the biggest and grandest theatre thus far, but it lacked one important ingredient: Roxy. Major Bowes had overdone everything and the theatre needed Roxy to trim away the excess opulence and turn it to elegance. So in 1922, shortly after the Capitol's disastrous opening, the partners stepped aside and surrendered to Roxy.

By that time Roxy had taken an interest in a new medium. Rather than bow to the power of radio, he transferred the Roxy charm to the microphone and personally conquered the airwaves. Recognizing the tremendous advertising potential of radio, and also looking for something to meet the competition from it, Roxy broadcast live the pre-movie music and comedy show from his Capitol theatre. His famed closing words, "God Bless You" made the vaudeville radio "gang" a welcome Sunday night visitor in millions of American homes.

In 1925 Roxy was lured away from radio by the prospect of building his own theatre with Herbert Lubin. He placed the Capitol Theatre as well as his radio gang back in the capable hands of Major Bowes and went on to build his dream. Every prior theatre had only been a rehearsal for "The Cathedral of the Motion Picture: The Roxy. "

Shortly after joining forces with Rothafel, Lubin realized he couldn't possibly raise the necessary capital to accommodate the impresario's grandiose plans and therefore sold his interest to William Fox for five million dollars. Down to the last detail of seating, sound, architecture, and awe-inspiring effect, the Roxy became the quintessential Movie Palace. Reporters who reviewed the opening night spectacle were too overwhelmed by the architecture to sufficiently describe it. As a result, they groped unsuccessfully for adequate adjectives.

Roxy called his lobby a rotunda; architect W. W. Ahlschlager and decorator Harold Rambusch were given the task of transforming the gigantic room into a "great bronze bowl." When Roxy envisioned his bowl, he saw gold. Three hundred plasterers were gathered to work their rococo magic on every available inch. The Roxy also utilized Renaissance details of gold filigree and vivid red. The rotunda was supported by twelve marble columns, and rose five stories above a magnificent oval rug which weighed over two tons, measured fifty-eight by forty-one feet, and cost $15,000. Amber glass windows, crystal chandeliers, and enormous urns decorated the immense 6,214-seat auditorium.

Housed within its colossal structure, the Roxy had a mammoth assemblage of accessories. The theatre came equipped with a musical library housing over 50,000 orchestral scores. There were washroom facilities for 10,000, as well as a hospital and two attendant nurses. There were five floors of dressing rooms, lodging for animals, and a radio broadcast studio. Roxy's world

came complete with his private health club that included a steam room and massage table. Whenever he chose to inspect the kingdom, Roxy took a secret passage from his office to a private box, and there surveyed his masterpiece.

On the night of March 11, 1927, the Roxy opened in triumph. The Marquise de la Falaise de la Coudraye, better known as Gloria Swanson, had married her Marquis just in time to see her picture, *The Love of Sunya*, open in a palace worthy of royalty.

In 1930, Roxy was granted another opportunity for immortality. A large portion of land in New York City had been leased from Columbia University by John D. Rockefeller, Jr. The Metropolitan Opera had originally intended to occupy the space, but when their plans failed, Rockefeller selected the Radio Corporation of America as the new tenant.

It was an obvious decision to select Roxy as overall director of the new theatre. He was then one of NBC's most famous radio stars, and NBC was owned by RCA. In addition, no one knew more about Movie Palaces than Roxy, and therefore no one else could possibly work the same magic at Rockefeller Center as had been realized at the Roxy. In January 1931, Rothafel resigned his position at his beloved namesake theatre and moved uptown with the Rockefellers to confront a fresh challenge.

The new structure was designed by The Associated Architects, an organization that included Raymond Hood and Edward Durell Stone. A competition was held to locate an interior designer worthy of Rockefeller Center. Several long-established and wealthy firms submitted plans. A little-known artist named Donald Deskey, who had just returned from *L'Exposition Internationale des Arts Décoratifs et Industriels Modernes* (the famous Paris exhibition which initiated the Art Deco movement) was an unlikely candidate, but his trip to Paris stood him in good stead.

Sidney Patrick Grauman put Movie Palaces in Movieland's capital city, Hollywood.

The knowledge he had gained coincided perfectly with the theme of Radio City Music Hall: humanity's progress in art, science, and industry.

At the age of thirty-five, with only $5,000 in the bank, Donald Deskey was awarded the prestigious commission. The choice proved a wise one, for even today Deskey's effort is recognized as an Art Deco masterpiece.

The interior of Radio City Music Hall is characterized by an elegant simplicity best seen in its enormous Grand Foyer. Measuring sixty feet in height and one hundred fifty feet in length, the enormous foyer is a perfect blend of mirrors, marble, gold leaf, and bronze. The magnificent mural which adorns the southern wall provides a harmonious complement to the overall decor.

Deskey experimented with the latest materials, such as Bakelite, cork, and aluminum, and his furniture represented the symmetrical perfection intrinsic to the Moderne movement. He hired the best artists and craftsmen available. Despite stringent budget controls, the overall construction cost of Radio City Music Hall exceeded seven million dollars.

Opening night was a classic Samuel Lionel Rothafel extravaganza. Amelia Earhart, Charlie Chaplin, William Randolph Hearst, Noel Coward, and Irving Berlin were just some of the celebrities occupying the 6,200 seats. Above them was a magnificent curved ceiling with a gracefully lit sunrise shimmering out from the proscenium arch. The theatre was spectacular, but something was wrong.

The show began forty-five minutes late, and even Ray Bolger, the Flying Wallendas, and the Roxyettes couldn't counteract the numbing excessiveness. There were nineteen separate vaudeville acts, and by the time the last had finished—at 2:30 a.m.—the performer was taking his bows before a half-filled auditorium.

Dwarfed by the magnificence of his theatre, Roxy stood in the rear of the auditorium surveying his colossal disaster. Only a few years before, he had scanned the Roxy Theatre with binoculars searching in vain for a pair of sleepy eyes. On the rare occasion that he spotted a bored customer, he personally interviewed him to find out what was wrong. On December 27, 1932, the defeated impresario didn't need binoculars to see that many had stayed only because they were too drowsy to get up and leave.

Roxy had violated one of his own basic laws. He had overdone everything. The entertainment was the best in the business, but it seemed to go on forever. The disappointment was devastating for Roxy. Already the victim of one heart attack, he was too weak to bear the reviews that hit the papers in the morning. Even before he read them, Roxy collapsed, a broken-hearted man.

Roxy had devised his entertainment format on the premise that movies were a thing of the past. He predicted that a classy group of vaudeville acts would eventually evolve as a substitute. Hoping to stay one step ahead, he fell miserably behind. When he was well enough to return to the theatre, he found movies were the entertainment focus, and he also found that he was an unwelcome employee. The strain increasingly damaged his health and on January 13, 1936, at the age of fifty-three, Roxy died. The times had moved past him, and his ideas were as obsolete as the Movie Palace would be within a few short years.

Radio City Music Hall survived its early reviews on the sheer beauty of the theatre. Despite the initial stage presentation, the architecture was recognized as magnificent. Ironically, the hall has recently been granted a new life based on Roxy's orginal concept of live performances. Crowds again marvel at the lavish showcase and enjoy top entertainment. The interior was extensively renovated in 1979. Sixty-foot gold curtains were re-woven, the fabrics were duplicated, the Wurlitzer organ was restored, and the graffiti were painstakingly scraped from Deskey's original murals.

Although the theatre has maintained his memory, Radio City Music Hall was never really a part of Roxy, unlike his triumph and favorite, the Roxy Theatre. His career was over when he left the palace which bore his name. For Samuel Lionel Rothafel, the Roxy Theatre would always symbolize his dream.

Now only the dream remains. In 1960, the magnificent pillars of the Roxy came crashing down in ruins to make way for an office building. Gloria Swanson, returning to the theatre she had helped open thirty-three years previously, walked with regal sadness through the rubble to wish a last farewell to Roxy and his greatest creation.

While Roxy was busy decorating Eastern cities with theatres, a little man with a thick mass of curly hair was dotting movieland's capital with appropriately fantastic palaces. Though hardly a rival, Sidney Patrick Grauman was perhaps Roxy's grandest imitator.

Grauman spent his early years traveling around the country in the company of his father's minstrel show. As a small boy he entertained workers in the gold-mining town of Dawson City, Alaska. Fed up with life on the road, young Sid persuaded his father to abandon the minstrel show and try their luck with the movies. They joined forces, and in 1906 Sid and David Grauman converted a store in San Francisco into an eight hundred seat theatre. It was a success, and the Graumans then opened an even larger theatre called the Imperial and combined movies with live vaudeville acts.

In 1917, Sid Grauman realized that since Hollywood was the entertainment capital of America it would seem only logical to build a Movie Palace there.

Recognizing his potential to be the West Coast Roxy, Grauman devised a unique entertainment format.

Whereas Roxy's stageshow was completely separate from the film, the Grauman "prologue" tied in directly with the theme of the film. Live western entertainment opened for cowboy movies; fashion shows preceded sophisticated romances.

The Million Dollar was Sid Grauman's first palace; its name referred to the value of the land plus the cost of construction. Predominately Spanish in motif, The Million Dollar utilized many other styles as well. In a triumph of fantasy over chronology and coherence, baroque structure blended with cubist decorations to create a setting inhabited by ancient warriors and pagan gods.

With the opening of the Million Dollar, Grauman intended to make Los Angeles' Broadway the Great White Way of the West. The theatre opened in 1917 with Charlie Chaplin, D. W. Griffith, Mack Sennett, and Cecil B. De Mille in attendance.

The Million Dollar is still standing, but its new name is "El Teatro Million Dollar." People wait hours to see the films, but now they're lined-up to see Cantinflas and Maria Lopez.

Moving still closer to the pulse of movieland, Grauman followed his next theatre, the Rialto, with an immense structure right in the center of Hollywood. The Egyptian Theatre was based on the architecture of ancient Thebes. The extensive use of hieroglyphics, sphinxes, barges, beetles, and Nubian slaves made a visitor feel as if he'd just entered the tomb of King Tut.

In 1923, Grauman was back downtown to build the Metropolitan. Designed by William Lee Woollett, the Metropolitan was constructed to resemble an ancient temple. Woollett believed that as the public was still somewhat disoriented due to the war, eclectic Movie Palace decor would best suit the mood of mental confusion. The result was bizarre yet uniquely beautiful. Woollett created an exotic and primitive effect by painting the wet plaster of the Metropolitan's walls with a fresco of an ancient ruin. As a substitute for the traditional chandelier, a black glass fixture was added to dramatically reflect a dazzling spectrum of colorful lights.

Grauman's next theatre represented the pinnacle of his career. The Chinese Theatre was for Grauman what the Roxy was for Rothafel. Designed by the firm of Meyer and Holler, the pagoda palace was authentically Chinese, down to the gong in the courtyard and the hand-woven rugs. A dramatic sixty-foot sculpture of intricately carved silver dragons dominated the ceiling.

On opening night, Hollywood Boulevard was buzzing. D. W. Griffith was master of ceremonies, and when he gave Mary Pickford the signal to start the show, she pressed a jade button and opened a theatre which has remained a major tourist attraction since 1927.

Even though Sid Grauman was recognized as a master showman, his greatest publicity scheme happened by accident. One afternoon just before opening night at the Chinese Theatre, Grauman took Norma Talmadge to watch the construction. When they arrived, Miss Talmadge unintentionally stepped in wet concrete. Grauman's eyes lit up; he asked Miss Talmadge to append her signature to her footprint, and a fifty-year-old tradition was begun.

When Grauman made the decision to build his palaces in Los Angeles, he was warned that because of the geographical layout, people would never go downtown to the theatre. Grauman proved them wrong. During the twenties and early thirties, the public attended the downtown and Hollywood theatres. It didn't matter if it was necessary to drive an extra thirty miles, the show was worth the distance.

Time, however, proved both Grauman and his critics wrong: Neither a theatre's design nor its location is enough to attract or discourage customers. Today it's the films themselves which draw the audiences.

The Architecture

Many fine architects contributed their skills to this flamboyant era. But the aesthetic quality of their work, like that of the early film directors, was often ignored by the cultural arbiters of the day. Many critics considered movies and their palaces to be, at best, extravagant curiosities and certainly not legitimate art forms. Movie Palace architects, however, turned this disapproval to their advantage and reveled in the artistic freedom allowed to renegades. Their unfettered creativity found a perfect outlet in these shrines to the imagination.

As the word "theatre" became obsolete and "palace" replaced it, two main styles of architecture emerged: The standard, or hard-top, was a more exotic version of the opera house and vaudeville theatre. The atmospheric theatre (invented by John Eberson), with its ceiling of twinkling stars and drifting clouds and its walls decorated in alfresco Mediterranean motifs, created the illusion that the film was being viewed under a night sky in a romantic setting.

The most famous hard-top architect was a Scotsman named Thomas W. Lamb. During his career he designed more than three hundred theatres. Lamb built his first Movie Palace in 1909, but his career gained momentum in 1913 when Henry Marvin commissioned him to design the Regent Theatre. That assignment set him upon a course which would run a close parallel to the early career of Samuel Rothafel.

The Regent allowed New Yorkers a hint of Movie Palace architectural wonders to come, and Lamb's arcaded Italian Renaissance facade was a sign to passersby that the days of the nickelodeon were gone for good.

Throughout his early career, Lamb was influenced by the eighteenth-century Scottish architect, Robert Adam. Adam was a neo-classicist who designed stately mansions throughout England. Adam drew upon influences from the Palladian movement, and his austere and elegant style was enhanced by an extensive

The San Francisco Fox was Thomas Lamb's great tribute to French Baroque architecture.

Courtesy Terry Helgesen

use of columns, domes, and arches. Adapting Adam's symmetric lines and classic ornamentation, Lamb created buildings of an overall beauty that was subtly magnificent without being ostentatious.

After the Regent, Lamb built the Strand Theatre on Broadway, featuring Corinthian columns and beautiful Wedgwood-inspired ceilings. The ceiling panels were painted in tones of blue and white and gracefully set into elaborate domes. The Rialto was Lamb's next adventure. Following this, he went to an Adamesque extreme with the Rivoli in 1917 and created on Broadway a terra-cotta replica of the Parthenon in Athens. Lamb's classical theatres included the Stanley in Philadelphia, the Loew's Orpheum in Boston, the Loew's State in St. Louis, and the Albee in Cincinnati.

Loew's Orpheum in Boston was built in 1916. It, too, featured the traditional grand marble staircase, and vaulted ceilings painted in the manner of Josiah Wedgwood's exquisite pottery. The Orpheum cost two million dollars, with $78,000 expended for marble.

Loew's State in St. Louis was built in 1924 and provided a glimpse of Lamb at his most elegant. The facade was characterized by gigantic columns and corner pilasters. The lobby was a wonderland of marble, fountains, and Corinthian columns. The foyer too, was ornate. In addition to deep brown walnut paneling, it was highlighted by a Palladian touch: A marble balustrade formed a window through which a mural of the sea was displayed. A graceful violet marble staircase with fluted Tuscan columns completed the foyer. The interior of the auditorium was distinguished by two magnificent paintings of the muses of drama and music, which were framed by Corinthian columns with blue and white Wedgwood bases.

Offering a preview of a style he would later develop more fully, Lamb designed the Albee in Cincinnati to combine the neoclassicism of Adam with the

exuberance of rococo. Its thirty bronzed and beveled glass doors formed an entryway obstacle course in eye-distracting opulence.

Then, apparently seduced by the flamboyance of the era, Lamb discarded the neoclassic, conservative mode and moved with gusto into the Italian baroque and flashy Louis XVI styles. No longer did he detail his theatres with tasteful Corinthian columns, but rather with cherubs, gold leaf, and lavish plaster swirls.

The Midland Theatre in Kansas City perfectly represented Lamb's de luxe period. In addition to being wildly extravagant, the Midland was innovative in its architecture and engineering. It contained the first cantilevered loge section as well as the first cooling, heating, and ventilating system of any theatre in the United States. The lush baroque/rococo interior required a crew of fifteen sculptors and over one hundred workmen to complete. The elegant antiques which filled it were acquired from the William K. Vanderbilt townhouse in New York City.

The Midland, once the personal favorite of theatre magnate Marcus Loew, went through many changes in the years following its construction in 1927. In the early sixties the palace, with its six and one-half million square inches of gold and silver leaf, was converted into a bowling alley. Then in 1964, at a cost of over $500,000, the Durwood theatre chain restored Lamb's eclectic details of Czechoslovakian cut-crystal chandeliers, Imperial Russian eagles, life-size cherubs, Corinthian columns, and golden peacocks.

Perhaps an even more flamboyant example of Lamb's de luxe period was the extravagant San Francisco Fox, decorated with fabulous antiques and paintings which the owner's wife, Eve Leo Fox, purchased in European marketplaces. Arriving on the tail end of the Movie Palace era, the Fox floundered for many years and was demolished in 1963.

John Eberson's Paradise Theatre in Chicago was demolished in 1956.

Courtesy Terry Helgesen

Not content with the baroque and Louis XVI styles, Lamb seemed determined to completely renounce his early Adam convictions. In 1929, he turned to Hindu, Persian, Chinese, and Spanish influences as inspiration for the Loew theatre chain in New York. Lamb decorated the Loew's State in Syracuse and the Loew's 175th Street and 72nd Street theatres in New York City with images of slaves, horses, elephants, Oriental royalty, as well as exotically jeweled and colored murals, pillars, and carpeting.

Lamb even ventured to duplicate John Eberson's atmospheric clouds in his 72nd Street Theatre. This enormous Siamese auditorium was laden with Aladdin lanterns, golden grilles, and Buddhas. The atmosphere created by the clouds was mysterious, and the bronzed incense burners gave the impression of an ominous and magical world. Built in 1932, Loew's 72nd Theatre had five dog kennels to service its patrons' pets and a beautiful Art Deco ladies' cosmetic room. In 1961, all this splendor was torn down to make room for an apartment building.

Whereas Thomas Lamb started traditionally and ventured into the flamboyant, there was never any question that John Eberson was a master of the exotic.

Eberson was the originator of the atmospheric "stars and clouds" theatre. An Austrian architect, Eberson knew instinctively that the American audience desired total fantasy. His first entry into architectural escapism was in 1922 with the Majestic in Houston, Texas.

Atmospheric theatres like the Majestic provided a truly unreal environment. Once inside their auditoriums, patrons would be magically transported outside once again, only this time they would find themselves magically seated in a Spanish patio, an Egyptian temple, a Persian court, or an Italian garden—all with a romantic night sky above.

Construction costs for an atmospheric theatre were much lower than those for the standard variety. The ceiling had a plain concrete surface on which nocturnal images were projected by a small machine called the Brenograph Junior. As visitors gazed upwards from their comfortable seats, wispy clouds seemed to drift across the concrete "sky." A plaster menagerie of gods, goddesses, trellises, entwining vines, stuffed birds, and other pastoral fantasies decked the walls.

As the first atmospheric theatre, the Majestic realized Eberson's dream of bringing the illusion of nature indoors through a perfect blend of lighting, color, and architecture. But Eberson also enjoyed breaking the carefully created mood with humorous anachronisms. He would momentarily disrupt the quiet tranquility of a clear, blue Italian Renaissance evening by projecting the image of a modern airplane flying overhead. Such gimmicks were made possible by variations of the Brenograph Junior cloud-making machine.

The Avalon Theatre in Chicago was Eberson's grandest jewel. Down to the last hand-made tile, the Avalon appeared to be an authentic Persian temple. High above the proscenium arch hung a huge cloth like a desert tent appearing to shelter the entertainers from the possibility of falling stars. There were lanterns, a minaret skyline, and a fountain with running water.

Eberson built over one hundred theatres and all the ornate columns, trellises, and statues he used in them were manufactured in his own plaster-cast empire known as the Michelangelo Studios. It produced some quite remarkable works. The Paradise Theatre in the Bronx, for example, contained statues inspired by those guarding the tombs of the Medici in Florence.

In addition to statuary and stuffed birds, Eberson's Uptown Theatre in Kansas City offered free parking plus an escorted trip to the parking lot by a uniformed attendant wearing white gloves. In 1939, this unique

Rapp and Rapp's Uptown Theatre in Chicago was the setting for many great Balaban and Katz stage presentations.

Courtesy Terry Helgesen

showplace copyrighted a new invention: "Fragratone." This aromatic delight released various perfumes from the air conditioning vents at moments of flowery passion in the film.

Although Eberson and Lamb stand out as the supreme Movie Palace designers, there were many other architects who sprinkled the American landscape with their temples, palaces, and twinkling stars.

The Chicago architectural firm of C.W. and George Rapp took the fantasies created by Eberson and Lamb even further. Based on their idealistic philosophy that in the splendid bliss of a Movie Palace an overabundance of glitter could unite all men, Rapp and Rapp constructed sanctuaries of illusion where the rich and poor could find respite together.

The Central Park was their first theatre. Opened in 1916, it gave Chicago its first Movie Palace and established the Rapp's employer, the Balaban and Katz organization, as the mid-western version of Roxy.

Dominating the city with the kind of theatres that demonstrated the high cost of fantasy, Rapp and Rapp brought all the splendor of the Orient to Chicago in the Oriental Theatre. Then they recreated Versailles near the Loop with the Chicago and Tivoli Theatres.

Built in 1921, the Chicago Theatre was the ultimate in French opulence, and in the traditional Rapp and Rapp style of excess, the Chicago had not one, but three box offices. The lobby contained crystal and bronze Pearlman chandeliers, and the auditorium walls were lined with majestic boxes. The interior of the theatre was decorated by Marshall Field and Company in tones of blue, red, and gold.

Rapp and Rapp's Ambassador Theatre in St. Louis presented a plush, Spanish carnival motif. As was true in all their theatres, Rapp and Rapp exaggerated the already mammoth dimensions. The Ambassador accomplished this with arches, vaults, a grand staircase with ornamental brass railings, and a forty-foot mirror to double the grandeur. The ceiling of the auditorium consisted of eleven silver leaf domes which when lighted gave the atmospheric effect of a silver sky.

A popular trend during this period was to build a theatre in one town and, if it was successful, recreate it in another city. C. Howard Crane's Detroit and St. Louis Fox theatres were examples of such twins. Created in the "Siamese Byzantine" style, these theatres were an unusual mixture of Moorish, Far Eastern, and Indian designs. The predominant chandelier lit up with 696 bulbs to reflect the prismatic wonder of 1,244 pieces of cut glass. The giant globe weighed two and one-half tons and cost $40,000.

The Fox Theatre in Atlanta, Georgia, stands out as definitely special, even considering the typically grandiose eclecticism of Movie Palace architecture. Islamic in motif, the Fox was a masterpiece in interior and exterior tile. The elaborately detailed exterior terraces doubled as fire escapes. The auditorium was equally ornate, and one would have more readily expected to find a turbaned worshipper on a prayer mat than an American housewife swooning over John Barrymore. Designed by P. Thornton Marye, the "Xanadu of Dixie" occupied a one-block area and offered a mecca of rococo rugs, Byzantine brick, baroque balconies, Egyptian art, and Arabic arches. Originally built as a Masonic hall called the "Yaarab Temple of the Ancient Arabic Order of the Nobles of the Mystic Shrine," it was financed to completion and converted into a Movie Palace by William Fox in 1929. The atmospheric effect was completed by an amazing decorative detail. The canopy ceiling which upon first glance appeared to be an enormous striped tent, was in actuality composed of plaster on a steel substructure. To add authenticity, a touch of brown mildew was painted in the center of the canopy.

Douglas Fairbanks' *Robin Hood* opened in this maze of hieroglyphics, Meyer and Holler's Egyptian Theatre.

Courtesy Terry Helgesen

In the Southwest, Aztec motifs enjoyed a vogue. The Phoenix Aztec Theatre, the Meyer and Holler Aztec Theatre in San Antonio, Texas, and the Mayan Theatre in Los Angeles were all designed under the spell of ancient Mexico.

Built by Morgan, Walls, and Clements in 1927, the Los Angeles Mayan featured an immense terra-cotta facade which was painted to resemble a Yucatan ruin. The innovative use of paints achieved an aged appearance which gave the impression that the Mayan Theatre had been excavated by archaeologists. The tiled lobby floor depicted a wooden carving from an ancient temple in Guatemala. Scenes from mythology covered the walls as sky gods, sun gods, firebirds, and worshipping Mayans blended with the colorful Aztec symbols. Additionally, the cantilevered ceiling provided a colossal illustration of a Mayan calendar centered on a sunburst chandelier.

Nautical motifs were also used to decorate the Movie Palace. The Avalon Theatre on Catalina Island, off the coast of Los Angeles, was built by Weber and Spaulding in 1929 to display all the wonders of King Neptune's paradise in addition to housing a gambling casino. The theatre was built in the Spanish style but with an overall Moderne interpretation. The undersea setting was highlighted by mermaids swimming along the ornate walls.

Benjamin Marcus Priteca, one of the most extravagant of Movie Palace architects, and S. Charles Lee, one of the most prolific, easily dominated theatre construction on the West Coast.

At the age of twenty-one Benjamin Priteca was commissioned by Alexander Pantages to design the original San Francisco Pantages. Mr. Pantages was Greek and insisted that Priteca's early theatres be designed according to the classical themes of his homeland. The Pantages theatres were distinguished by superb acoustics as well as triple domed ceilings and elaborate stained art-glass panels.

One of Priteca's early theatres was the Coliseum in Seattle. Built in 1916, its original decor combined classical and Oriental detailing with Egyptian murals and bas relief busts of Renaissance nudes. During its heydey the Coliseum housed thirty canaries in its upstairs foyer, and the auditorium ceiling twinkled with likenesses of the Big Dipper and the North Star.

Abandoning the Greek motif, Priteca adopted a Spanish theme for the San Diego Pantages in 1923. He followed that with a magnificent Italian Renaissance theatre designed to replace the original San Francisco Pantages. Priteca designed the Seattle Orpheum in 1927 and decorated it with ornate brick, marble, and bronze. In 1928, Priteca constructed the Paramount Theatre in Seattle. The grand foyer was four stories high, and its two gold and crystal chandeliers reflected the lavish ceiling and beige and black marble interior.

The Hollywood Pantages was Priteca's most famous theatre. For many years the Academy Award ceremonies were held within its auditorium. This magnificent theatre with its golden goddesses and walnut and marble details was also once the setting for a performance by Sergei Rachmaninoff on piano with orchestra under the direction of Leopold Stokowski. In 1949, the theatre was purchased from the Pantages family by RKO, then owned by Howard Hughes who kept an office above the theatre. The Pantages has been maintained as a successful musical comedy theatre, and, although it has been substantially remodeled, the Hollywood Boulevard landmark is still recognized as an elegant entertainment showcase.

S. Charles Lee, Priteca's fellow West Coast architect, received his early training with the Chicago firm of Rapp and Rapp. Throughout his long career, Lee built or reconstructed over four hundred theatres

The Beverly Hills Fox was Benjamin Marcus Priteca's finest Art Deco theatre.

Courtesy Terry Helgesen

The Entertainment

throughout the world. Believing that the show began on the sidewalk, he insisted that the marquee, box office, and sign tower harmonize to form an appealing facade. And, because the lights came on so often, between the live acts and film reels, it was also necessary for the interior to be equally spectacular.

The Los Angeles Theatre, Lee's most palatial, opened in 1931 at a cost of two million dollars. Charlie Chaplin donated an additional sum in order to insure that the theatre would be complete for the world premiere of his classic *City Lights.*

Its opulent decor depicted the life and historical times of Louis XIV. The auditorium had a magnificent coffered ceiling with an abundance of murals in the style of the French Renaissance. Two magnificent staircases met at a giant Carrara marble fountain. Surrounded by ten sculpted dolphins, water cascaded gracefully down six tiers and into a basin.

The Los Angeles Theatre enabled Lee to experiment with his early equivalent of closed circuit television. He devised a system of prisms that transmitted the film from the projection booth down to a small screen in the main lounge. Here, amidst beautiful French antiques, a late viewer could watch the film without disturbing the audience. The theatre also had a sound-proof "crying room" where mothers could deposit their shrieking infants into the able hands of a supervisor. Without the distraction of her child, a woman was better able to concentrate on the eyes of John Gilbert.

S. Charles Lee gave up his art in 1948, when it became obvious that a new and less charming era was upon us. Today most theatre architects focus more on technical than aesthetic challenges. Their buildings are functional, not exuberant, and their legacy to the future is that modern version of the store show—the shopping center cinema.

Driving down the Broadways of America on a Saturday night, we are drawn to the swirls of neon that signal to the imagination, "Stop here for a good time, a night on the town, and a really great movie!" The magic of the marquee has long helped to transform mundane daytime business streets into boulevards of glaring excitement at night. Even from its earliest days, the marquee advertised the show and protected its waiting customers from rain or sun.

The show of lights alone represented something special to early moviegoers. Even if they didn't venture inside, the light display gave them an unusual and free experience. The sign on the Rialto lit up to reveal one of the greatest lightbulb firework shows in New York. Rising from the legendary 1916 theatre, a spectacular pinwheel showered stars while an eagle flapped its wings against the background of the American flag. In the midst of this gigantic sparkler were the letters R-I-A-L-T-O.

The box-office, or bijou, was another hallmark of the Movie Palace. Bijou in French translates as jewel, and indeed these tiny ticket boxes were small jewels of their parent movie houses. The history of the bijou goes back to the days of the peep show when a lady in a booth dispensed tickets while regulating the flow of traffic into the theatre. Just as the marquee brought in business, the box office also became a focal point on the exterior of the theatre. The box offices were elaborate structures in themselves, and often previewed the architectural masterpiece inside.

Already primed for something out of the ordinary, guests would most certainly be dazzled upon entering the foyer, lobby, or rotunda. They stepped into a world whose stature made their problems seem eminently forgettable. Just when a visitor became completely awed, an usher would appear, dressed like a military officer, and say, "At your service!"

S. Charles Lee's Los Angeles Theatre is still gorgeous and still showing movies.

Courtesy Terry Helgesen

Samuel Rothafel was the supreme commander of all Movie Palace ushers. His troops at the Rialto wore costumes trimmed in gold. When it became necessary to direct a late customer to his seat, the knight in shining armor would show the way with a mother-of-pearl tipped stick that glowed in the dark.

Young men were proud to be called "usher." Working in a prestigious downtown theatre was like belonging to an exclusive club. Upon acceptance into the fraternity, a new "brother" received a medallion and pin, and a pair of spotless white gloves. Sports and other recreation were provided for off-duty hours. In New York, basketball tournaments were played between inter-theatre teams on a court in the basement of the Loew's King. An usher's efficiency inspired respect. His demeanor and uniform were usually military. Not all ushers looked ready for combat, however. The squad at the Valencia Theatre in Baltimore wore Spanish bullfighter costumes and colorful silk shirts. A six-piece mariachi band serenaded the matadors as they went about their duties.

A customer in a Movie Palace was always intended to feel special, even when visiting the restrooms. A trip to the ladies lounge was an experience not to be missed. It was almost worth going a few hours early so as to have ample time for primping in a parlor worthy of an Egyptian princess or a lady of the royal court. Even the most "ordinary" Movie Palace rest rooms contained exquisite antiques.

A mechanical bird chirped from its cage outside the ladies room at the Valencia, and the individual toilet stalls had ornate gates of entry. The lounge at the Ambassador Theatre in St. Louis was a reproduction of Madame Pompador's salon at the Palace of Fontainbleau in France. A $7,500 gold-leaf piano stood directly outside Madame's salon. The ladies lounge in the Los Angeles Theatre had sixteen individual rooms,

each decorated with a different shade of marble. And, should the film prove dull, there was a full-time manicurist to shine your nails.

Often these shrines to vanity were situated at the bottom of an elegant staircase. The outer lounge would be filled with plush furniture, silk wallpaper, and mirrors galore. After lounging a sufficient time, a lady could saunter back upstairs unconcerned that her escort might be fuming, for the men's rooms were as fabulous as the women's.

Beautiful tiles, carved screens, lanterns, and ornate furniture decorated the Persian-style men's lounge at the Avalon Theatre in Chicago. At Radio City Music Hall the gents could relax in one of Donald Deskey's Art Deco mini-museums. The smoking room on the second mezzanine contained original Deskey furniture and a beautiful mural entitled "Nicotine" which illustrated the varied story of tobacco on a unique aluminum background.

After receiving the full treatment of military cadets and plush lounges, the thoroughly pampered patron would enter the main auditorium for phase two of the show: the live entertainment and movie. Seated in a comfortable, plain-colored chair (Roxy believed that colorful upholstery would clash with the clothes of the patrons and therefore ruin the overall effect of the theatre), the audience would settle back and wait for further magic to begin.

A complete symphony orchestra was generally too expensive for a small city palace, so the Mighty Wurlitzer organ assumed full musical responsibilities. Set in the orchestra pit, or in a niche just off the stage, the Wurlitzer was so enormous that it dwarfed the person at the keyboard.

The organ was like the voice of a deity directing the

An elevator transported patrons from the basement to the balcony of G. Albert Lansburgh's Los Angeles Orpheum Theatre.

emotions of the audience and the actors on the silent screen. This incredible machine, originally called a "unit orchestra," was invented by Robert Hope-Jones around 1908 and manufactured by the Wurlitzer Company. Hope-Jones transformed the common church organ into the Mighty Wurlitzer of the Cathedral of the Motion Picture.

At the push of a colorful button, the sound of a glockenspiel, snare drum, banjo, tambourine, or sleigh bell would travel through thousands of pipes and out to an enraptured audience.

In addition to musical instruments, organists could call upon canaries, fire engines, hurricanes, or steamboat whistles. Their chords could produce the musical passions of love, anger, hatred, and jealousy.

The Movie Palace enabled the average theatregoer to experience classical music, opera, and occasionally ballet. The orchestra often consisted of accomplished musicians and eminent conductors. Eugene Ormandy was an early maestro at the Capitol Theatre who educated his audiences to the loftier sounds of Beethoven, Tchaikovsky, and Brahms.

Roxy enforced his high-brow tastes by treating his audiences to the classics, while at the same time providing standard favorites such as patriotic numbers and chorus girls. A Sid Grauman prologue might include a glamorous fashion show with beautiful girls in bathing suits or lavish gowns. Balaban and Katz, the great entrepreneurs of Chicago, believed that the stage show should follow a theme but have no relation to the motion picture. In conjunction with showman Frank Cambria, they presented stage shows as lavishly costumed and detailed as the Rapp and Rapp theatres in which they played.

Many great acts appeared on the Movie Palace stage. Franchon and Marco's Sunkist Beauties and the Chester Hale Girls provided audiences with memorable

entertainment, but perhaps the greatest show of them all, and one which is still going strong, is the Radio City Music Hall Rockettes with their legendary legs.

The original "Rockets" were formed by Russell Markert and consisted of sixteen dancers. Roxy merged two troupes of Rockets and called the thirty-two girls the Roxyettes. When they moved from the Roxy Theatre to Radio City Music Hall, their name was changed to the Rockettes. Known the world over for their incredible precision and glamour, they inspired many a young girl to dream of joining them. And now, with the recent revival of Radio City Music Hall, the little girls who dream today have a better chance at becoming the Rockettes of tomorrow.

Many well-known film personalities got their start in vaudeville. Comics such as George Burns and Bob Hope once told jokes live on a Movie Palace stage.

There were acrobats, animal acts, evangelists, and magicians. In addition to the featured film, an audience could sing along with the music and watch travelogues and newsreels.

There was so much to choose from. Even if customers didn't enjoy half the show, they still got their money's worth and left convinced that they'd definitely been entertained. The marquee, the architecture, the stage show, and the movie—all had been created for them.

Pix Theatre–Hollywood, California

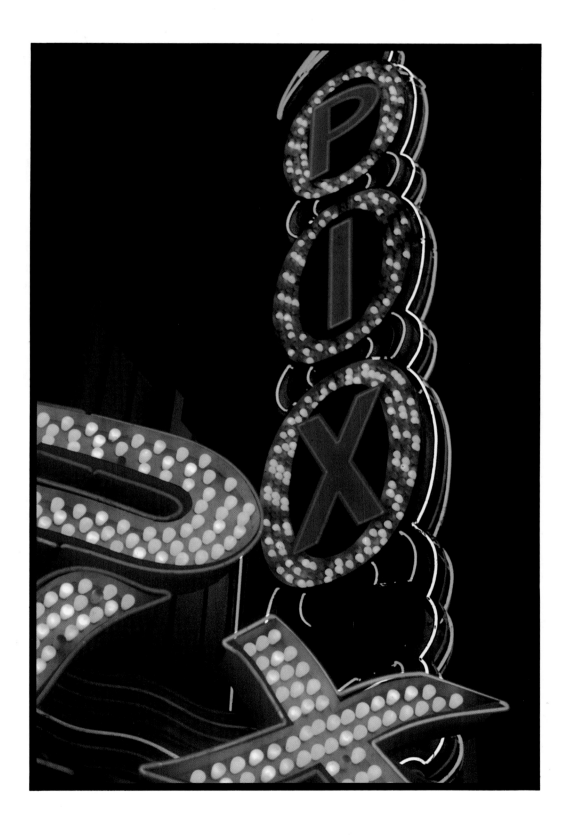

Loma Theatre–San Diego, California

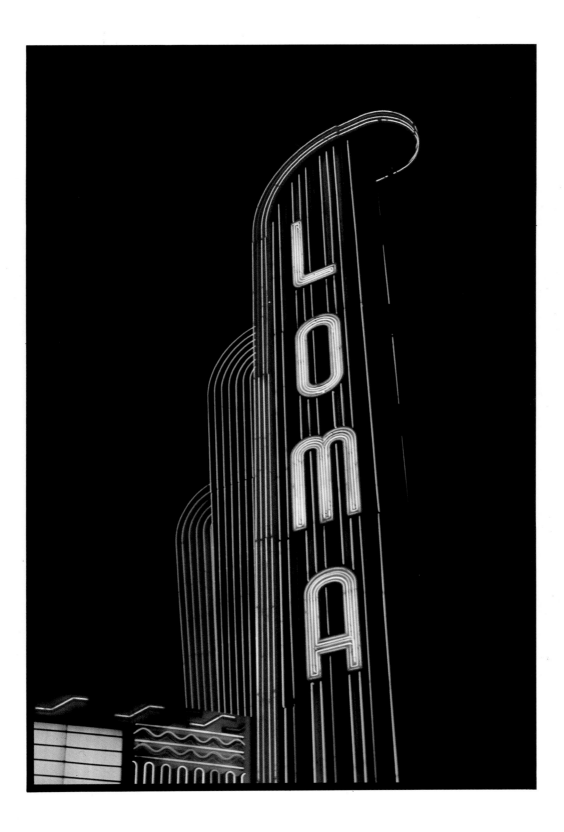

Rialto Theatre–Los Angeles, California

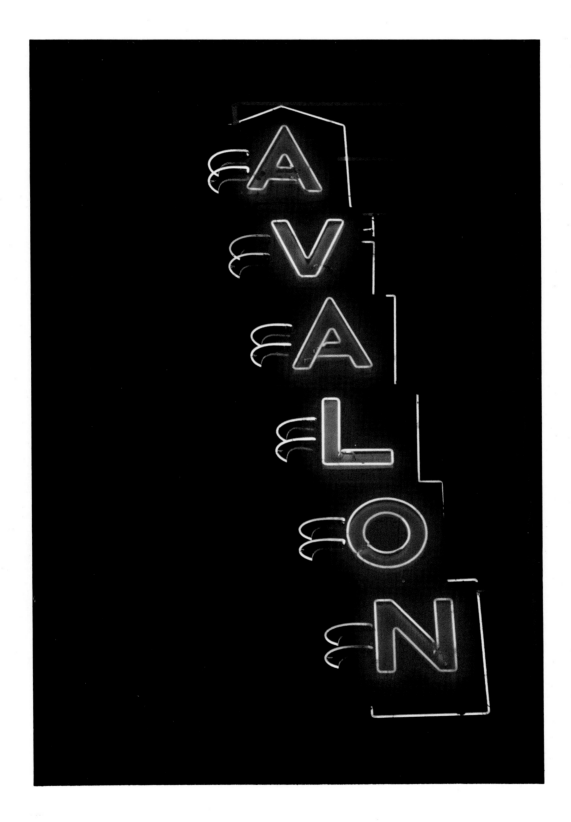

1. Belmont Theatre–Belmont Shores, California
2. Rialto Theatre–Los Angeles, California

3. Broadway Theatre–Portland, Oregon
4. State Theatre–Los Angeles, California

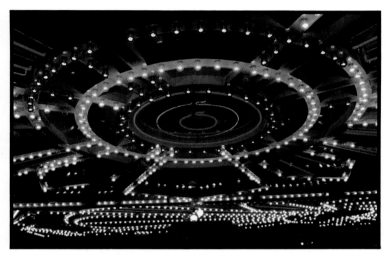

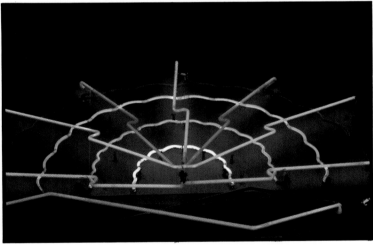

◀ Laurelhurst Theatre–Portland, Oregon

Orpheum Theatre–Los Angeles, California

Garmar Theatre–Los Angeles, California

Loyola Theatre–Los Angeles, California

Star Theatre–Oceanside, California

1. Alabama Theatre–Houston, Texas
2. Texas Theatre–San Antonio, Texas

3. Fremont Theatre–San Luis Obispo, **California**
4. Pantages Theatre–Hollywood, California

Palace Theatre–Long Beach, California

Chicago Theatre–Chicago, Illinois

Orpheum Theatre–Los Angeles, California

Palace Theatre–Los Angeles, California

Plaza Theatre–San Diego, California

Pix Theatre–Hollywood, California

◀ Centre Theatre–Denver, Colorado

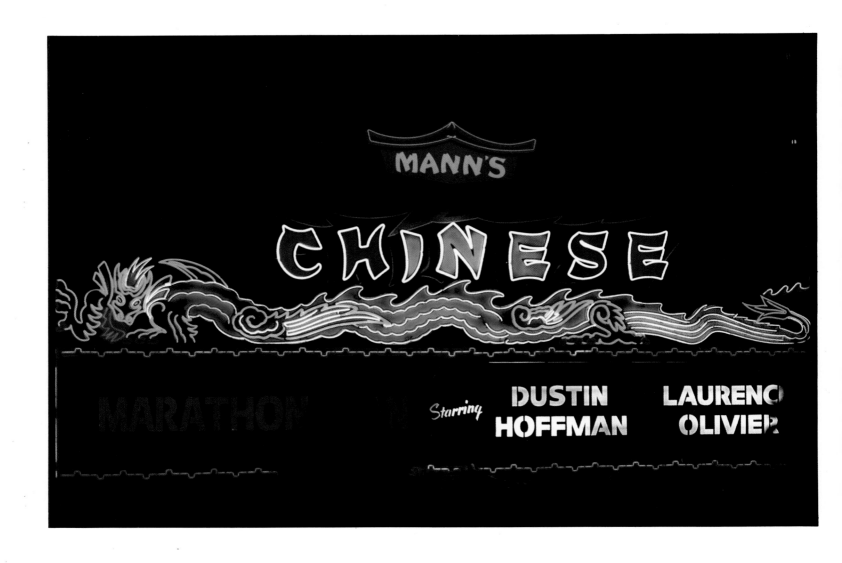

Mann's Chinese Theatre—Hollywood, California ▶

◄ Mann's Chinese Theatre, exterior detail

Mann's Chinese Theatre
1. Interior
2. Interior detail, lobby

3. Exterior detail
4. Courtyard

Mann's Chinese Theatre, courtyard details

Mann's Chinese Theatre, courtyard

Avalon Theatre–Catalina Island, California

Loyola Theatre—Los Angeles, California

Chicago Theatre–Chicago, Illinois

Orpheum Theatre–New Orleans, Louisiana

Gordon Theatre–Hollywood, California
Fox Theatre–Atlanta, Georgia

El Portal Theatre–Los Angeles, California
Spreckels Theatre–San Diego, California

Warner Theatre–Huntington Park, California
Plaza Theatre–San Diego, California

El Rey Theatre–Los Angeles, California
Wardman Theatre–Los Angeles, California

Wiltern Theatre–Los Angeles, California

Westlake Theatre–Los Angeles, California
Mayan Theatre–Los Angeles, California

Colonial Theatre–Richmond, Virginia
Tower Theatre–St. Louis, Missouri

State Theatre–Long Beach, California
Village Theatre–Los Angeles, California

Aberdeen Theatre–Aberdeen, Washington
Cameo Theatre–Los Angeles, California

Hollywood Theatre–Hollywood, California

Fox Theatre—Atlanta, Georgia; facade

Aragon Theatre–Chicago, Illinois; facade

Mayan Theatre–Los Angeles, California; exterior detail

1. Mayan Theatre–Los Angeles, California; facade
2. Radio City Music Hall–New York, New York; exterior detail

3. Nortown Theatre–Chicago, Illinois; exterior detail
4. Pantages Theatre–Hollywood, California; exterior detail

1. Westlake Theatre–Los Angeles, California; exterior detail
2. Loyola Theatre–Los Angeles, California; neon detail

3. Fox Theatre–Beverly Hills, California; showcase detail
4. Alameda Theatre–San Antonio, Texas; exterior wall detail

Gordon Theatre–Hollywood, California; exterior terrazzo

Exterior terrazzos   ▶
1. Roxy Theatre–Los Angeles, California
2. Magnolia Theatre–Los Angeles, California
3. Los Angeles Theatre–Los Angeles, California
4. Fremont Theatre–San Luis Obispo, California
5. Theatre demolished, terrazzo intact–Los Angeles, California
6. Coronado Theatre–Pasadena, California
7. Plaza Theatre–San Diego, California
8. Alex Theatre–Glendale, California

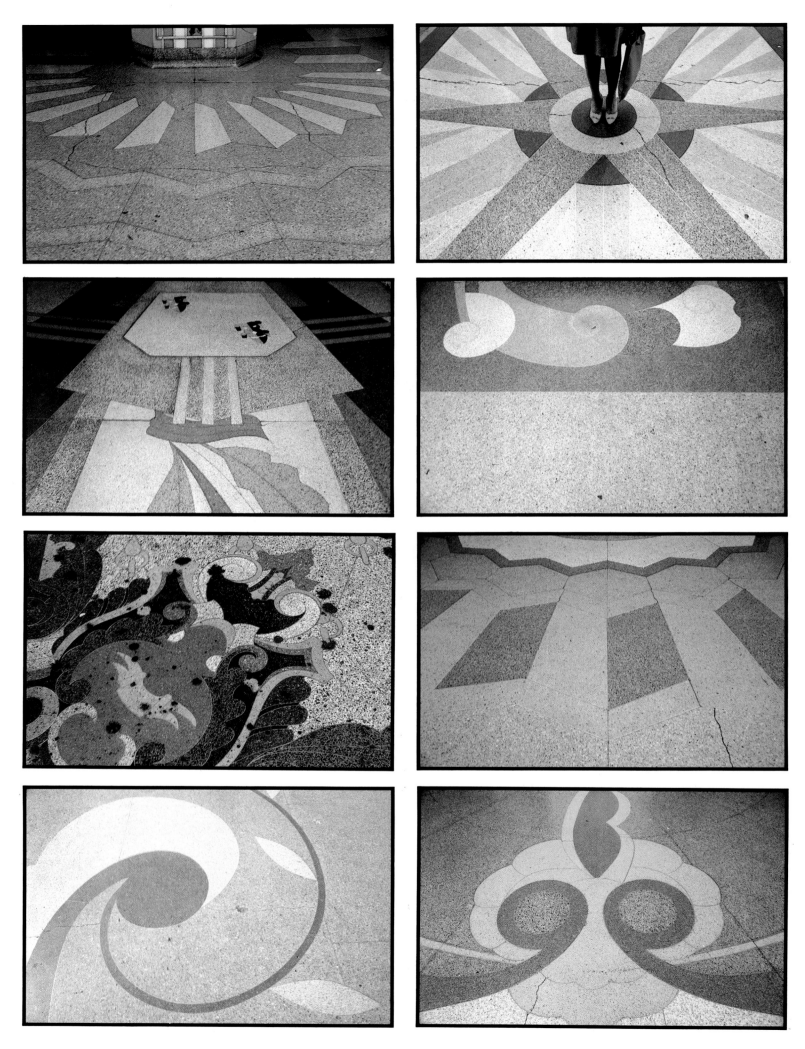

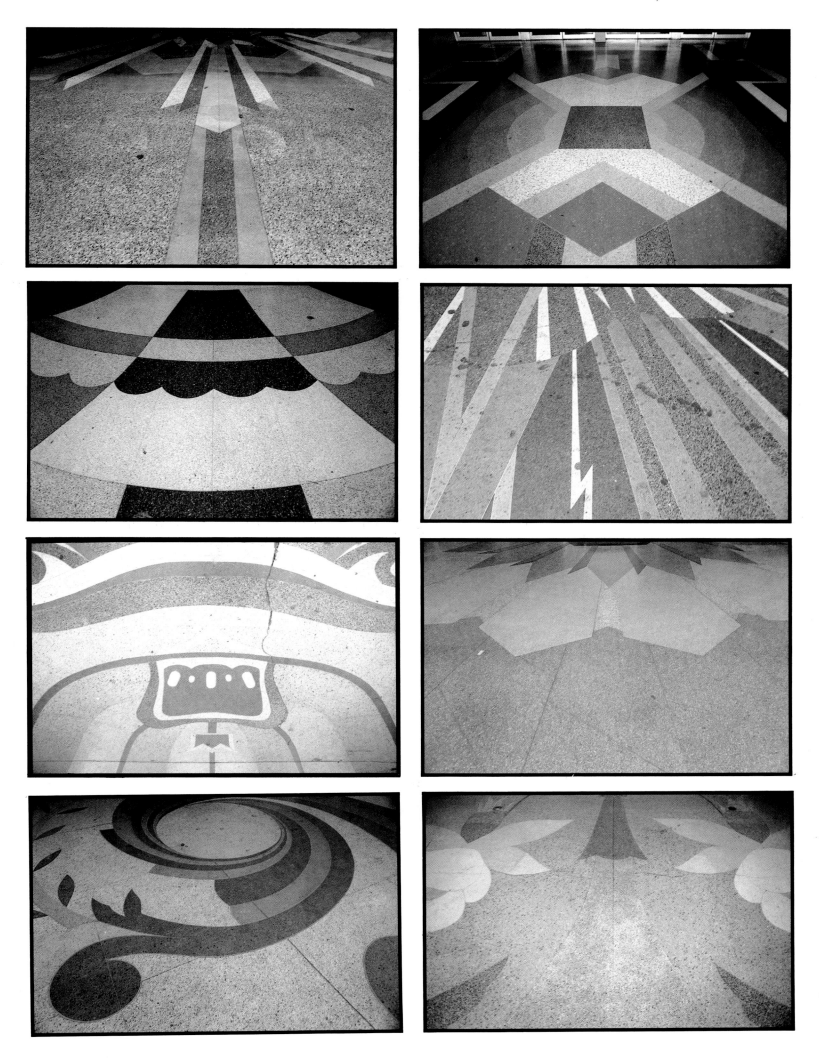

Crown Theatre–Pasadena, California

◀ Exterior terrazzos.

1. Warner Theatre–Huntington Park, California
2. Boulevard Theatre–Los Angeles, California
3. Alameda Theatre–San Antonio, Texas
4. Centre Theatre–Denver, Colorado
5. Lankershim Theatre–North Hollywood, California
6. Theatre demolished, terrazzo intact–Los Angeles, California
7. Wiltern Theatre–Los Angeles, California
8. Tower Theatre–Los Angeles, California

Crown Theatre, curtain

Avalon Theatre–Catalina Island, California

Centre Theatre–Denver, Colorado

Midland Theatre–Kansas City, Missouri

Fox Theatre–Atlanta, Georgia

Paramount Theatre—Aurora, Illinois

Kimo Theatre–Albuquerque, New Mexico

1. Auditorium
2. Ceiling detail
3. Wall detail, interior
4. Exterior detail

5. Lobby interior
6. Lobby detail
7. Interior detail
8. Exterior facade

▶

Byrd Theatre–Richmond, Virginia

Warner Theatre–Erie, Pennsylvania

1. Alameda Theatre–San Antonio, Texas
2. Pantages Theatre–Hollywood, California; Lobby

3. Powell Hall–St. Louis, Missouri; Lobby
4. Pantages Theatre–Hollywood, California

1. Mayan Theatre–Los Angeles, California
2. Aztec Theatre–San Antonio, Texas

3. Savoy Theatre–Boston, Massachusetts
4. Texas Theatre–San Antonio, Texas

Paramount Theatre–Oakland, California

Paramount Theatre, Lobby interior ▶

Paramount Theatre, Auditorium ▶

Paramount Theatre
1. Auditorium detail

2. Lounge detail

Paramount Theatre
1. Lounge
2. Lower lobby carpet
3. Lounge
4. Wall detail

Moore Egyptian Theatre–Seattle, Washington; lobby detail

Midland Theatre–Kansas City, Missouri; lobby detail

1. Midland Theatre–Kansas City, Missouri; lobby
2. Saenger Theatre–New Orleans, Louisiana; auditorium

3. Loew's Theatre–Richmond, Virginia; auditorium
4. Oriental Theatre–Chicago, Illinois; lobby

Paramount Theatre–Denver, Colorado; auditorium detail

1. Uptown Theatre—Chicago, Illinois
2. Savoy Theatre—Boston, Massachusetts

3. Mayan Theatre—Los Angeles, California
4. Ohio Theatre—Columbus, Ohio

1, 2, 5, 6.
Avalon Theatre–Catalina Island, California
3, 4, 7, 8.
State Theatre–Cleveland, Ohio

Nortown Theatre–Chicago, Illinois; upstairs lobby, ceiling

Powell Hall–St. Louis, Missouri; interior detail

Midland Theatre–Kansas City, Missouri; lobby ceiling ▶

1. Savoy Theatre–Boston, Massachusetts
2. Orpheum Theatre–Los Angeles, California

3. Ohio Theatre–Columbus, Ohio
4. Midland Theatre–Kansas City, Missouri

Warner Theatre–Erie, Pennsylvania; moulding detail

1. Fox Theatre–Atlanta, Georgia
2. Coliseum Theatre–Seattle, Washington
3. Nortown Theatre–Chicago, Illinois
4. Savoy Theatre–Boston, Massachusetts

Ohio Theatre–Columbus, Ohio

1. Warner Theatre–Erie, Pennsylvania
2. Orpheum Theatre–Los Angeles, California
3. Mann's Chinese Theatre–Hollywood, California
4. Los Angeles Theatre–Los Angeles, California

EPILOGUE: THE SURVIVORS

A visit to a Movie Palace powder room was worth the price of admission to fantasyland.

Julius Shulman

By the end of the twenties, the steady stream of moviegoers had dwindled. Occasionally, a new Movie Palace would appear, but gradually most potential developers reconsidered this type of investment.

In 1926, Warner Brothers Studio was on the verge of bankruptcy. Due to several poor real estate speculations and a generally bad turn-out at the box office, the ailing corporation was desperate.

At about the same time that Warner Brothers was searching for a miracle, a variation of the Vitascope was introduced. The "Vitaphone" not only projected movies, it projected movies that talked. On August 7, 1926, at the Manhattan Opera House in New York, the Vitaphone made its debut. This early "talkie" featured John Barrymore and the sounds of the New York Philharmonic in an overly dramatic version of *Don Juan*.

Taking what was considered an enormous risk, Warner Brothers invested its last resources in the Vitaphone; the reputed "gimmick" of talking movies saved Warner Brothers and the motion picture industry but signaled the beginning of the end for the Movie Palace.

Al Jolson's *The Jazz Singer* contained only a few words of dialogue and three songs, but in October of 1927 it started a revolution which transformed many businessmen into overnight millionaires and forced many silent film stars into humiliating obscurity.

Despite the fact that "talkies" sent the public back to the theatres, the cost of reconstructing an auditorium to accommodate sound was very expensive. An average tab of $30,000 for sound equipment was very steep for the pocketbook of a struggling Movie Palace owner.

Actors, too, were forced to change. Prior to talking movies, acting was defined by facial expressions. Within one year however, every major motion picture "talked" and both actors and theatre owners had to make the transition or find another business.

The new enthusiasm sparked a momentary resurgence for Movie Palaces. For example, the San Francisco Fox opened spectacularly in 1929, but by 1931 it closed.

Movie Palaces were the indulged offspring of affluence; the end of abundance marked them for extinction. Although during the Depression people needed the movies to relieve their worries, they couldn't often afford the lavish escape of the Movie Palace. They attended cheap no-frills theatres or remained home and listened to the radio or read books and magazines.

During World War II the palaces again experienced a temporary revival when the public came to see military films and revues inspire patriotism and Humphrey Bogart generate intrigue. But by 1948, the masses were saving their money to buy a television set, the strange-looking box that was to give the *coup de grâce* to the Movie Palace. What wishful-thinking theatre owners dismissed as a fad rapidly became the future of popular entertainment.

When the movie industry faltered in 1915, D.W. Griffith had come to the rescue. In 1929, the producers were ready with talkies. But when television exploded onto the scene in 1948, Hollywood was empty-handed.

Although the movie industry is still attempting to recover from the crisis that television caused, most Movie Palaces have succumbed. Many fell to the wrecker's ball; parking lots and apartment buildings now occupy their sites. Others were pathetically hybridized into roller skating rinks, supermarkets, miniature golf courses, and pornographic film parlors.

Beginning in the late sixties, a movement has grown to save the remaining Movie Palaces. Happily, the mammoth efforts of local citizens have paid off and many great old palaces have been granted last-minute reprieves. Due to their low cost and magnificent acoustics, many of these theatres have been converted into symphony halls.

Once a famous preview house where producers and stars watched private screeenings, the Academy Theatre in Inglewood is now a church. As the Movie Palace evolved into the movie theatre, the functional replaced the flamboyant.

Julius Shulman

In 1968, Rapp and Rapp's St. Louis Theatre was renovated and its name changed to Powell Symphony Hall. Instead of movies, the theatre, which was fashioned after the chapel of Louis XIV at Versailles, is now filled with the music of the St. Louis Symphony Orchestra.

Two million dollars were spent on the restoration of the enormous auditorium. New theatre seats were added, the marble floors were refurbished, a few minor alterations were made to accommodate orchestral sound, and $88,000 was spent on twenty-four karat gold-leaf paint to retouch the original details. Violinist Isaac Stern honored the great old theatre by performing on the opening night of its new life.

In 1927, Loew's Penn Theatre opened in Pittsburgh. A genuine Rapp and Rapp masterpiece, with its Venetian ceiling, rococo plaster detail, bronze and crystal chandeliers, and silk damask draperies, it was built in anticipation of a long and profitable career. But it, too, was eventually caught in the long decline of the Movie Palace. After a brief attempt at musical comedy in 1967, the theatre closed.

Recognizing a potential home for the Pittsburgh Symphony, the Howard Heinz Foundation stepped in, saved the great theatre and designated it as a cultural center where music, ballet, and opera would be performed. In order to meet the specifications demanded by a symphony hall, major changes were made. It was necessary to redesign the foyers and much of the auditorium. However, the lavish cartouches, domes, and Rapp and Rapp details still remain after its overall facelift. Loew's Penn is now the Heinz Hall for the Performing Arts.

Another Rapp and Rapp success story is the Paramount Arts Centre in Aurora, Illinois. That grand old building has been restored to its original Art Deco splendor. Even the colorful marquee has been reinstalled as a positive symbol of survival. The Arts Centre promises

to be the focal point of Aurora's lavish new Civic Center. Films, Broadway shows, and concerts by the Fox Valley Symphony Orchestra will celebrate this recycled masterpiece.

Several of Thomas Lamb's theatres have also been given a new chance at life. In 1971, the Loew's Ohio Theatre was converted into a permanent home for the Columbus Symphony Orchestra. That regal monument to Lamb's de luxe period was resuced by the "Save-The-Ohio Committee." Even after the demolition contract was signed, the Columbus Association for the Performing Arts refused to give up. They summoned additional funds and at the last moment the theatre was saved. Now, in addition to the symphony orchestra, classic movies are run with an organ accompaniment.

The magnificent mirrors, marble, and crystal were all polished-up on Thomas Lamb's Savoy Theatre to welcome the Opera Company of Boston. After much searching, the company realized that the golden baroque palace would prove an ideal setting for the elegance of opera.

In 1970, the Oakland Paramount faced a grim future. Timothy Pflueger's Art Deco palace waited on death row while appeals were made to save its magnificent gold and mosaic renderings of "man's progress." The Oakland Symphony claimed the theatre in 1973, and for a purchase price of one million dollars saved it from extinction. The original furniture, carpets, and draperies were re-created in almost identical fabrics, and the auditorium with its radiant gold plasterwork and grilles was retouched with gold leaf. The zig-zag details on the interior as well as the gigantic exterior mosaic with its ominous puppeteer dangling the strings of man's existence have remained intact, and now symphonies, ballets, popular concerts, and even an occasional movie are displayed on the historic and scenic premises.

Only one year after it's grand opening in 1931, G. Albert Lansburgh's Los Angeles Wiltern Theatre closed. It reopened in 1936, but its future remains uncertain.

Courtesy Terry Helgesen

Playhouse Square in Cleveland, Ohio, symbolizes a true miracle for the Movie Palace. Standing side by side, four separate examples of architecture are being restored to comprise the theatrical complex; Thomas Lamb's elegant State Theatre is now a supper club. Surrounded by James Daugherty's colorful murals and Lamb's Wedgwood ceilings, patrons dine and once again enjoy live entertainment. The Ohio Theatre is unfortunately in a state of severe disrepair. Following the catastrophes of fire, flood, and the final insult of being painted red, the original beauty of the theatre has been almost completely obliterated. Nevertheless, Playhouse Square supporters have hopes that one day the auditorium will house chamber music, stage, and ballet performances. C. Howard Crane's Allen Theatre is again showing movies; and the most splendid of the four theatres, Rapp and Rapp's Palace, will be a spectacular symphony hall. Its tapestries, inlaid ceilings, marble urns, statuary, and staircases—all enriched with elaborate French details—will provide an ideal setting for classical music.

The saving of these great theatres has been a tremendous accomplishment, but one that unfortunately cannot succeed in cities where a performing arts center is not currently needed. While some Movie Palaces are situated in cities where they can be converted, the majority of theatres face an uncertain future.

Many palaces are in the same situation as G.A. Lansburgh's Wiltern Theatre in Los Angeles. This beautiful Art Deco structure with its faded green facade now sits with an enormous price tag of over six and one-half million dollars. Its function as a Movie Palace is no longer profitable, but its property value has soared. No significant offers have been made to rescue it, and if it were destroyed, the value of the land it sits on would increase even more.

Downtown property is so precious that buildings on it must generate huge incomes to justify their existence

economically. If not, tremendous pressures exist to tear them down and put up structures that will produce the maximum cash flow. Only a small group of citizens—seldom, of course, including the owners—advocate historic preservation instead of high profits.

Now that population and theatres have shifted to the suburbs, the public no longer needs these lovely anachronisms. Even their role as fantasy castles has been usurped. Futuristic buildings such as the Hyatt Hotel in San Francisco and the Bonaventure Hotel in Los Angeles have taken over this function. These ultra-modern "palaces" transport people's imaginations into the twenty-first century, toward space technology and science fiction.

It is an unfortunate American trait that as we charge ahead to the future, we often disavow our past and bury any evidence which reminds us of our heritage.

Inevitably, many Movie Palaces will be torn down. With each one that falls, we forfeit a portion of ourselves and erase a moment of our youth that can never be regained.

Movie Palaces provided fantasy, laughter, and entertainment in a setting of splendor that makes modern theatres look depressingly drab. They were the cathedrals in which for the first time humanity was joined in mass electronic communication. The transformation of human awareness by media that began there is one of the most far-reaching developments of the century. By demolishing its origins, we impoverish ourselves.

As we eliminate our past, we justify our loss with the magic word "progress". This destruction breeds a frightening callousness which distorts our values. The Movie Palace is a vital symbol of the social and cultural history of America. If we destroy it, we will have made an irretrievable mistake.

NOTES ON THE THEATRES

Avalon Theatre—Catalina Island, California
1929, Weber & Spaulding
Fantastically nautical in motif, the Avalon Theatre and Casino made an unusual statement in Art Deco. Built for the Wrigley family on Catalina Island, the Avalon's walls displayed an eclectic blend of mermaids, explorers, and undersea deities.

Chicago Theatre—Chicago, Illinois
1921, George and C.W. Rapp
The Chicago Theatre is one of the last surviving Rapp and Rapp Movie Palaces in Chicago's Loop district. Decorated by Marshall Field and Company, the elegant theatre was famous for its lavish Balaban and Katz stage productions. Six stories of dressing rooms once flanked either side of the colossal stage. Many of the crystal and gold fixtures have been replaced with plastic and bronze. Although they lack the original lustre, these recent repairs offer a positive indication that the Chicago Theatre will survive.

Chinese Theatre—Hollywood, California
1927, Meyer and Holler
Perhaps the most famous Movie Palace in the world, the Chinese Theatre still attracts tourists to its legendary courtyard. The masterpiece of showman Sid Grauman, it was recently purchased by the Mann theatre chain. The Chinese Theatre's carved red doors, grand pagodas, and ornate murals have made it the center of movieland's capital: Hollywood.

Fox Theatre—Atlanta, Georgia
1929, P. Thornton Marye
The Fox Theatre is a celebration of Eastern design. The main auditorium was built to resemble a Moorish courtyard, while the interiors of the lounges were inspired by the discovery of Tutankhamen's tomb in 1922. Complete with doornobs carved in the likeness of a pharaoh's mask, the theatre is a landmark worthy of its name, the Fabulous Fox.

Kimo Theatre—Albuquerque, New Mexico
1927, Carl Boller
A monument to Indian culture, the Kimo's enormous walls are decorated with elaborate murals illustrating scenes from Indian folklore. Rain clouds, longhorn skulls with lightbulb eyes, Indian blankets, war shields, birds, and mystic symbols are used in abundance.

Mayan Theatre—Los Angeles, California
1927, Morgan, Walls, & Clements
Taking ornate complexity one step beyond gold, the Mayan Theatre is a mosaic extravaganza of ancient geometric patterns. Mayan symbolism covers every available inch, taking the form of entwining serpents, celestial symbols, ancient headdresses, and ceremonial gods. The blend of primitive colors gives the Mayan Theatre the faded authenticity of an ancient temple in Mexico.

Midland Theatre—Kansas City, Missouri
1927, Thomas W. Lamb
This cherubic wonderland of crystal, gold, and marble was for a period a bowling alley. Prior to its restoration in 1964, the Midland had been converted into a variety of establishments, none of which respected the integrity of its splendid past. Rich with furnishings from the W.K. Vanderbilt town house in New York, the Midland has received a modernizing face-lift which successfully restored the elegance of its chandeliers and statuary.

Ohio Theatre—Columbus, Ohio
1928, Thomas W. Lamb
A fourteen-year-old Judy Garland sang at the Ohio Theatre in 1938, and although celebrities such as Milton Berle, Jean Harlow, and Jack Benny also appeared there, not even its illustrious history could save it from the threat of a wrecker's ball in 1969. Through the heroic efforts of a group of dedicated citizens, the theatre was spared, and now its golden figurines and brocade panels greet the audiences of the Columbus Symphony Orchestra.

Orpheum Theatre—Los Angeles, California
1926, G. Albert Lansburgh
Spanish and Mexican films are shown today amidst this lavish Louis XIII style palace. Solid bronze doors open into a lobby ablaze with five gold, bronze, and crystal chandeliers. The auditorium is dominated by a ten-foot hand painted iris decorating the stage curtain. Built at a cost of 1.9 million dollars, the Orpheum was a popular showcase for such stars as Sophie Tucker and Lionel Hampton.

Paramount Theatre—Aurora, Illinois
1931, C.W. and George Rapp
A cascade of two thousand roses thrown from an airplane greeted the Paramount's opening night patrons. "Aurora's Most Precious Jewel" was an Art Deco masterpiece that featured an adjacent rock garden and waterfall. Reopened in 1978, this beautifully restored theatre is now the major attraction of Aurora's Center for the Performing Arts.

Paramount Theatre—Denver, Colorado
1930, T.H. Buell & Company
To welcome the magnificent Paramount Theatre to Denver, its citizens gave an appropriately spectacular party. The ceremonies began with an explosive fanfare of aerial fireworks, while inside the theatre visitors inspected an enormous floral arrangement which Jeanette MacDonald reportedly hand-picked and had flown in from Los Angeles just in time for the opening of her picture. Never lacking in gimmicks for its patrons, the Paramount sponsored an opening night contest. Each customer was invited to give a candid appraisal of the festivities. The reviewer who wrote the most constructive, albeit complimentary, critique was awarded a one hundred dollar diamond ring.

Paramount Theatre—Oakland, California
1931, Timothy L. Pflueger
The Paramount Theatre is a beautiful example of a restored Movie Palace. For its reopening in 1973, the carpets, auditorium fixtures, seats, carpets, draperies, and metal and glass details were duplicated to match the originals. The result is a splendid Art Deco home for the Oakland Symphony Orchestra.

Texas Theatre—San Antonio, Texas
1926, Robert Boller
In the typically lavish Movie Palace style, this "Western Rococo" theatre captured the old Spanish influence in Texas. For only eighty-five cents, a visitor could sit beneath a star-lit sky in a palatial Spanish patio and be entertained.

Wiltern Theatre—Los Angeles, California
1931, G. Albert Lansburgh
Opening nights such as the gala at the Wiltern Theatre perpetuated the glittery aura which surrounded Hollywood in the thirties. Two grand staircases crossed over the street and into the theatre. Amidst the sparkle of electric flowers, the arriving celebrities crossed over the bridge and into a mass of reporters and fans. The fate of this lavish Moderne theatre is uncertain today, but while it stands, the familiar green terra cotta facade with its majestic lines and swirling lights signifies a faded yet splendid past.

BIBLIOGRAPHY

Francisco, Charles. *The Radio City Music Hall: An Affectionate History of the World's Greatest Theater.* New York: E. P. Dutton, 1979.

Griffith, Richard, and Mayer, Arthur. *The Movies.* New York: Simon & Schuster, 1957.

Hall, Ben M. *The Best Remaining Seats.* New York: Clarkson N. Potter, Inc. 1961.

Hampton, Benjamin B., *History of The American Film Industry From Its Beginnings to 1931.* New York: Dover Publications, Inc., 1970.

Jacobs, Lewis. *The Rise of the American Film.* New York: Teachers College Press, 1967.

Knight, Arthur. *The Liveliest Art.* New York: Mentor Books, 1957.

Macgowan, Kenneth. *Behind The Screen.* New York: Delacorte Press, 1965.

Marquee, Quarterly Journal of the Theatre Historical Society, 1968–1979. P.O. Box 101, Notre Dame, Indiana 46556.

McCoy, Donald R. *Coming of Age.* London: Penguin Books, 1973.

Shannon, David A. *Between The Wars: America 1919–1941.* Boston: Houghton Mifflin Company, 1965.

Sharp, Dennis. *The Picture Palace.* New York: Frederick A. Praeger, 1969.

United States Department of the Interior, National Park Service, *National Register of Historic Places Inventory,* Nomination Forms.

INDEX OF THEATRES

Color photographs are indicated by roman type, black and white and text references by italic.